Table of Contents

Introduction 1

Executive Summary 3

Vulnerabilities Identified 5

    Filings on Mortgage Brokers 5

    Appraisal Fraud 5

    Vulnerabilities in Specified Mortgage Products 6

        Trend for Suspected Fraud in Cash-Out Refinance Loans 6

        Trend for Suspected Fraud in Stated Income/
        Low or No Document Loans 7

        Home Equity Lines of Credit 8

Fraudulent Activities and Red Flags 9

    Overview of Fraudulent Activities 9

    Commonly Reported Variations of Mortgage Fraud 12

    Elaborate Mortgage Fraud Schemes 14

Protective Measures 19

    Effective Fraud Detection Measures Used by Filers 19

    Other Protective Measures 20

**Trends and Patterns in Total SARs Reporting
Mortgage Loan Fraud** 21

    Characterizations of Suspicious Activity 24

    Primary Federal Regulators 26

    Top Filing Institutions 27

    Fraud Locations 27

    Individual Taxpayer Identification Number (ITIN) 34

Findings Observed from Sampled Narratives 37

    Types of Fraud 37

    Loan Types 40

    Early Payment Default 41

    Stated Income/Low Document or No Document Loans 43

    Fraud Detection 43

Securities and Futures Industries (SAR-SFs) 45

Conclusion 47

Introduction

Following a large increase in depository institution Suspicious Activity Report (SAR) filings on mortgage loan fraud, the Financial Crimes Enforcement Network (FinCEN) issued a report in November 2006 describing trends and patterns shown in SARs reporting suspected mortgage loan fraud filed between April 1, 1996 and March 31, 2006.[1] FinCEN has continued to monitor these reports. This analysis updates the previous report by reviewing SARs filed between April 2006 and March 2007.

---

1. "Mortgage Loan Fraud: An Industry Assessment based upon Suspicious Activity Report Analysis," see http://www.fincen.gov/MortgageLoanFraud.pdf.

Executive Summary

I n calendar year 2006, financial institutions filed 37,313 SARs citing suspected mortgage loan fraud, a 44% increase from the preceding year, compared to a 7% overall increase of depository institution SAR filings. One reason for this increase may be that lenders are increasingly identifying suspected fraud prior to loan approval and reporting this activity. Suspected fraud was detected prior to loan disbursements in 31% of the mortgage loan fraud SARs filed between April 1, 2006 and March 31, 2007, compared to 21% during the preceding ten years.

Total SAR filings in 2006 on suspected mortgage loan fraud, when divided by the subject's state address,[2] showed the greatest increases in Illinois (75.80%), California (71.29%), Florida (53.04%), Michigan (51.50%), and Arizona (48.73%).[3]

Mortgage brokers initiated the loans reported on 58% of the SARs sampled for this report. SAR reporting includes examples of brokers acting both as active participants in the reported fraudulent activity, and as intermediaries that did not verify information submitted on the loan application.

---

2. An increase in the number of subjects does not directly correlate into increased transactions. Since real estate transactions involve multiple parties, SARs frequently list multiple subjects in a single report. Some increases in reported subjects result from filers completing SARs more accurately or more thoroughly.
   Similarly, as some SARs indicate multiple subjects living in two or more states, these particular SARs may be included in multiple state totals. Consequently, total state filings, when listed by the subject's state, do not match the total number of SARs filers completed during the reviewed period.

3. These percentages represent the increase in SAR filings between 2005 and 2006. In this report, when percentages are in parenthesis, they are taken from a statistically representative sample unless noted otherwise, as here. Also, as many SARs contain multiple categories, such as subjects and activity types, some statistical tables and information contained in this report may exceed 100 percent.

Reports of suspected identity fraud and identity theft[4] associated with mortgage loan fraud continued to increase for the period reviewed. Reports of suspected identity theft in conjunction with mortgage loan fraud increased 95.62% over the previous study. Cases of suspected identity fraud were predominantly associated with fraud for housing.[5] Victims of identity theft have had their properties encumbered with loans or property titles fraudulently transferred, effectively having their homes stolen.

Filers specified that loans were subprime in 79 SARs (0.19%) for the reviewed period. Without this specification, it is not possible to determine whether mortgages described in the remaining SARs were subprime loans.

Sources for this Report

- Filing trends and patterns were identified based on data fields contained by all Suspicious Activity Reports (SARs) filed, where filers indicated mortgage loan fraud as a suspected activity.

- Additional filing trends and patterns were identified based on a statistically representative sample of SARs, where filers indicated mortgage loan fraud as a suspected activity.

---

4. For the purpose of this report, identity fraud was defined as the unauthorized use of a social security number issued to another individual or use of an invented social security number for the purpose of obtaining credit. Because the perpetrator used his/her true personal identifiers (i.e., name, address, and date of birth), there was no apparent attempt to steal another person's identity. Identity theft involved an attempt to obtain credit using another person's identity. The distinction made between identity fraud and identity theft is intended solely for the purpose of this report, and is not intended to establish legal definitions of these terms.

5. Mortgage loan fraud can be divided into two broad categories: fraud for housing and fraud for profit. Fraud for housing generally involves material misrepresentation or omission of information with the intent to deceive or mislead a lender into extending credit that would likely not be offered if the true facts were known. Fraud for housing is generally committed by home buyers attempting to purchase homes for their personal use. In contrast, the motivation behind fraud for profit is money. Fraud for profit involves the same misuse of information with the intent to deceive or mislead the lender into extending credit that the lender would likely not have offered if the true facts were known, but the perpetrators of the fraud abscond with the proceeds of the loan, with little or no intention to purchase or actually occupy the house. Suspicious activity reporting confirms that fraud for profit is often committed with the complicity of industry insiders such as mortgage brokers, real estate agents, property appraisers, and settlement agents (attorneys and title examiners).

Vulnerabilities Identified

Filings on Mortgage Brokers

A growing number of SARs report that mortgage brokers initiated the fraudulent loan applications. Filers are increasingly listing mortgage brokers as subjects in these SARs.

Figure 1 depicts a three year growth trend for total mortgage fraud comparing SAR filings and those reporting mortgage brokers as subjects. SARs reporting mortgage brokers as subjects comprise over one quarter of the total mortgage loan fraud SARs filed for the period between April 1, 2006 and March 31, 2007.

Figure 1

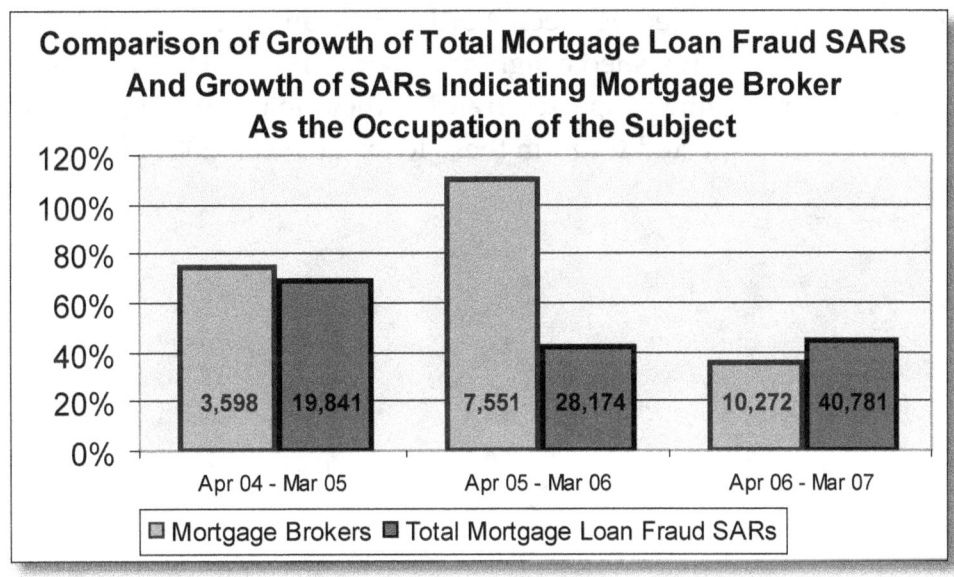

Appraisal Fraud

Reports of fraudulent appraisals continue to increase in SARs reporting mortgage loan fraud. Filers of nearly 13% of the narratives sampled for this report suspected appraisers as participants in the reported fraud. This represents an increase of two percentage points from the 11% reported in the 2006 FinCEN Mortgage Loan Fraud report. All fraudulent flipping[6] and nearly all other organized fraud schemes that were reviewed relied on fraudulent appraisals. A small number of sampled narratives reported the fraud was conducted through the theft of licensed appraisers' identity and license information. The increase in reporting of appraisal fraud and theft of licensed appraiser information underscores the value of independent verification of appraisal documentation.

Vulnerabilities in Specified Mortgage Products

Although many SAR narratives did not identify the mortgage product involved in suspected mortgage loan fraud activities, some associated trends and vulnerabilities were deduced from those narratives that did specify the mortgage product. A small number of narratives specified that loans were subprime.[7]

Trend for Suspected Fraud in Cash-Out Refinance Loans

Filers identified "cash-out refinance loans"[8] in 3.35% of the SARs reporting suspected mortgage loan fraud filed between April 1, 2006 and March 31, 2007. Over the past six years, the study revealed a significant growth in the number of depository institution SARs reporting suspected fraud in these loan products. There was a nearly 53% increase in suspected fraud in these loans between 2005 and 2006.

---

6. Property Flips: Property is purchased, falsely appraised at a higher value, and then quickly sold. What makes property flipping illegal is that the appraisal information is fraudulent. The schemes typically involve fraudulent appraisals, doctored loan documents, and inflation of the buyer's income.

7. For the period April 1, 2006 through March 31, 2007, 79 SAR narratives (0.19% of total filings) specified suspected fraudulent loans were subprime. Other SAR narratives do not provide sufficient details to make this determination.

8. A cash-out refinance loan is a refinanced loan granted for an amount greater than what the borrower owes on the prior loan. The additional amount of the refinance is funded by existing equity.

Figure 2 depicts this trend and projects the number for 2007.[9]

Figure 2

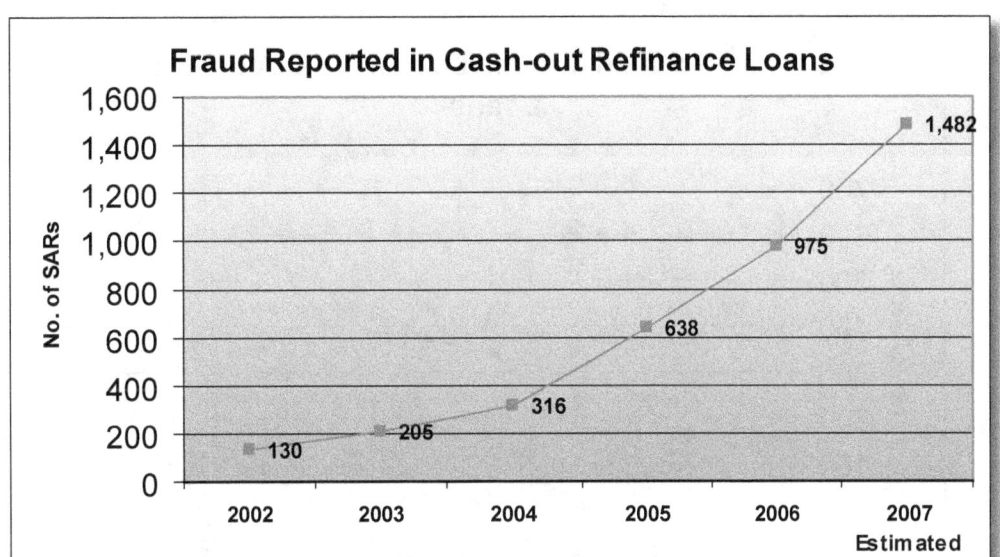

Trend for Suspected Fraud in Stated Income/ Low or No Document Loans

Filers specified that the mortgage product was a stated income, low or no document loan in 1.55% (633) of all SARs filed for suspected mortgage loan fraud between April 1, 2006 and March 31, 2007.[10] This represented nearly a 69% increase in loans thus specified from the previous one year period (375).

In the smaller sample reviewed, sixty-nine (3.9%) narratives specified the mortgage product was a stated income or a low or no document loan. Filers reported the suspected fraud was detected prior to loan financing on 18.84% of the reports for these mortgage products. In comparison to other loans identified in the sample, filers reported that they detected the suspected fraud prior to loan funding in 33.52% of full document purchase loans.

---

9. Projection is based on increases observed in comparisons of 1st quarters 2006 and 2007.

10. "A 'No Doc' loan is one in which extensive documentation of income, credit history, deposits, etc., is not required because of the size of the downpayment, usually 25% or more. Theoretically, the value of the collateral will protect the lender." FDIC, *Risk Management Manual of Examination Policies, Section 9.1 - Bank Fraud and Insider Abuse*, http://www.fdic.gov/regulations/safety/manual/section9-1.html.

Figure 3 provides a three year reporting trend for these mortgage products.

Figure 3

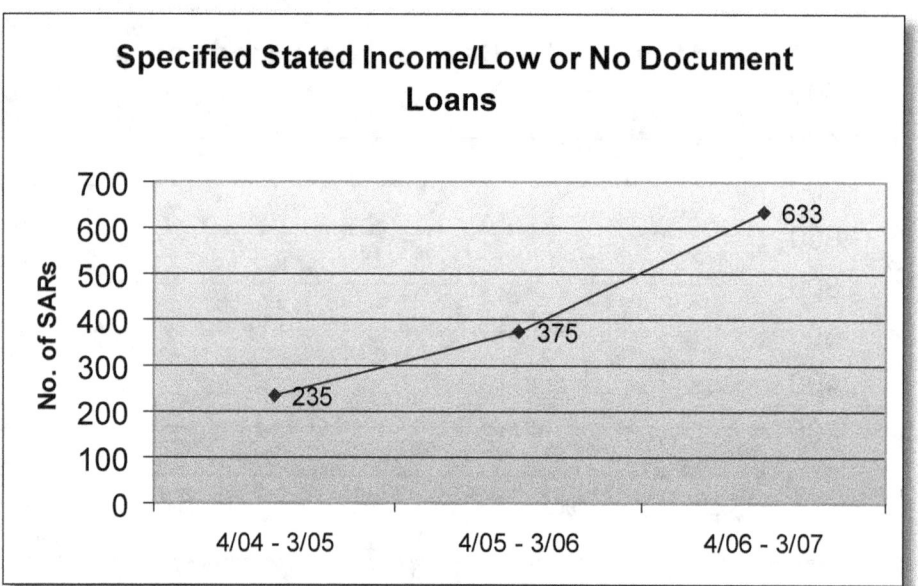

Home Equity Lines of Credit

Filers identified suspected fraud in home equity lines of credit on 1,492 (3.66%) of the SARs reporting mortgage loan fraud that were filed between April 1, 2006 and March 31, 2007. Over 61% of the suspected fraudulent home equity loans identified in the sampled narratives were classified as fraud for profit.

Fraudulent Activities and Red Flags

Overview of Fraudulent Activities

A sample of 1,769 depository institution SAR narratives was reviewed to identify additional trends and patterns reported in those narratives. The sampled SARs were reviewed to determine the types of activity and participants reported in the narratives.

Figure 4 provides the types of suspected fraudulent activities identified in the narratives.[11]

FIGURE 4

ACTIVITIES REPORTED IN SAMPLED SAR NARRATIVES		
Activity	No. of SARs	% of Sampled SARs
Misrepresentation of income/assets/debts	761	43.02%
Forged/fraudulent documents	496	28.04%
Occupancy fraud	255	14.41%
Appraisal fraud	232	13.11%
ID fraud	180	10.18%
Straw buyers	100	5.65%
ID theft	61	3.45%
Flipping	48	2.71%

11. In this chart, percentages may exceed 100 percent, as many SAR narratives include descriptions of multiple fraudulent activities.

Figure 5 provides a comparison of activity type by fraud type,[12] i.e. fraud for profit or fraud for housing.[13]

FIGURE 5

REPORTED FRAUDULENT ACTIVITY BY TYPE OF FRAUD				
Type of Activity	*Fraud For Profit*	*Profit % of Activity*	*Fraud For Housing*	*Housing % of Activity*
Misrepresentation of income/ assets/debts	239	31.41%	519	68.20%
Forged/fraudulent documents	97	19.56%	395	79.64%
Occupancy Fraud	241	94.51%	14	5.49%
Appraisal Fraud	140	60.34%	77	33.19%
Straw buyers	83	83.00%	15	15.00%
ID Fraud	6	3.33%	174	96.67%
ID Theft	61	100.00%	0	0.00%
Flipping	48	100.00%	0	0.00%

Figure 6 provides a comparison of the reported activities and participants reviewed in the sample.[14]

12. Not all SAR narratives provide sufficient details to determine if the activity appears to be fraud for housing or fraud for profit. Consequently, totals in Figure 5 are sometimes lower than totals in Figure 4.

13. For a fuller discussion of fraud for profit and fraud for housing, see page 37.

14. Most of these SARs include multiple subjects; totals do not reflect SAR volume (see Table 4 for SAR totals).

FIGURE 6

REPORTED FRAUDULENT ACTIVITY BY PARTICIPANT

Participant	Misrepresentation of income/assets/debts	Forged/fraudulent documents	Occupancy Fraud	Appraisal Fraud	Straw buyers	ID Fraud	ID Theft	Flipping
Appraiser	47 (6.18%)	16 (3.23%)	42 (16.47%)	215 (92.67%)	25 (25%)	1 (less than 1%)	3 (4.92%)	48 (100%)
Borrower	663 (87.12%)	412 (83.06%)	179 (70.20%)	91 (39.22%)	69 (69%)	171 (95%)	25 (40.98%)	28 (58.33%)
Builder	1 (less than 1%)	1(less than 1%)	1 (less than 1%)	4 (1.72%)	0	0	0	2 (4.17%)
Correspondent Lender	15 (1.97%)	4 (less than 1%)	3 (1.18%)	4 (1.72%)	2 (2%)	3 (1.67%)	0	1 (2.08%)
Insider (loan officer)	3 (less than 1%)	11 (2.22%)	4 (1.57%)	6 (2.59%)	3 (3%)	1 (less than 1%)	1 (1.64%)	1 (2.08%)
Investor	47 (6.18%)	5 (1.00%)	51 (20%)	22 (9.48%)	11 (11%)	1 (less than 1%)	0	7 (14.58%)
Mortgage Broker	488 (64.13%)	338 (68.15%)	158 (61.96%)	113 (48.71%)	66 (66%)	72 (40%)	39 (63.93%)	33 (68.75%)
Realtor	9 (1.18%)	4 (less than 1%)	4 (1.57%)	6 (2.59%)	4 (4%)	0	3 (4.92%)	3 (6.25%)
Seller	12 (1.58%)	8 (1.61%)	20 (7.84%)	26 (11.21%)	21 (21%)	0	0	14 (29.17%)
Settlement Services (includes attorneys and notaries)	12 (1.58%)	9 (1.81%)	4 (1.57%)	6 (2.59%)	4 (4%)	1 (less than 1%)	1 (1.64%)	2 (4.17%)

Commonly Reported Variations of Mortgage Fraud

Activities identified through a narrative analysis of the sampled SARs follow.

- Misrepresentation of income/assets/debts (43.02%). Material misrepresentation of income, assets, or debts was seen in both reports of fraud for housing (68.20%) and fraud for profit (31.41%). The suspected fraudulent loans were identified during post loan audits (56.37%); pre-funding reviews (24.44%); and upon loan defaults (15.90%). The reported activity involved fraudulent misrepresentation of employment and income and/or failure to disclose all debts or assets, such as additional real properties owned. These suspected misrepresentations resulted in higher debt to income ratios than considered acceptable, and would likely have precluded the loan issuance if reported accurately. Early payment defaults were reported in 5.12% of these narratives. Mortgage brokers initiated the loans on 64.13% of these reports. Forged/fraudulent documents (15.64%) and occupancy fraud (13.53%) were the most commonly reported activities in conjunction with misrepresentation of income, assets, or debts.

- Forged/fraudulent documents (28.04%). Filers reported submission of fraudulent W-2s, tax returns, verifications of deposit; verifications of rent; credit reports; and forged signatures on loan documents submitted to support income and assets. This activity was seen in fraud for housing (79.64%) and fraud for profit (19.56%). Mortgage brokers initiated the loans on 68.15% of the reports describing this activity. The suspected fraudulent activity was detected during pre-loan fund reviews (52.42%); post loan audits (31.05%); loan defaults (9.88%); and victims reporting forged signatures (3.83%).

- Occupancy fraud (14.41%). SARs reporting misrepresentation of the borrower's intent to occupy the property as a primary residence most frequently were associated with fraud for profit (94.51%). Generally, this misrepresentation was perpetrated in order to obtain a more favorable finance rate. Real estate investors participated in occupancy fraud for profit in 20% of these reports. A small percentage of the reports involving occupancy fraud (5.49%) described individuals acting as straw buyers for family members in order to help them obtain property. Mortgage brokers originated the loans involving suspected occupancy fraud on 61.96% of these reports.

- Appraisal Fraud (13.11%). Narratives indicating appraisal fraud described suspected fraud for profit in 60.34% and fraud for housing in 33.19% of filings. Generally the suspected fraud was committed through the use of inappropriate comparable properties to inflate property evaluations; inaccurate descriptions of the subject properties (failure to cite deficiencies or needed repairs); theft of a licensed appraiser's license number, or forgery of licensed appraiser's signature. In addition to appraisers, participants in loans where reviewed SARs indicated suspected appraisal fraud included: borrowers/investors (48.71%); mortgage brokers (48.71%); sellers (11.21%); loan settlement providers (including attorneys, and notaries) (2.59%); insider loan officers (2.59%); and correspondent lenders (1.72%).

- ID Fraud (10.18%). Identity fraud, the unauthorized and illegal use of another person's Social Security Number or a fraudulent (invented) Social Security Number not yet issued by the Social Security Administration, was nearly always classified as fraud for housing. Mortgage brokers reportedly originated 40% of the loans that were reported for identity fraud. Borrowers requested a change of the Social Security Number associated with their loans on 7.26% of these reports, thereby highlighting a likely identity fraud. Individuals who were associated with an ITIN[15] after obtaining a loan with a Social Security Number were identified on 17.22% of these reports. Filers identified the use of an ITIN prior to loan funding on 67.74% of the reports.

- Straw buyers (5.65%). Straw buyers were used in both fraud for profit (83%) and fraud for housing (15%) schemes. In the cases of fraud for housing, filers described individuals acting as straw buyers to help family and friends obtain property. Filers noted that mortgage brokers initiated the loans on 66% of narratives describing straw buyers. Many of the reports described individuals acting as straw buyers who failed to disclose all of their assets and liabilities, such as additional properties and mortgages they held.

- ID Theft (3.45%). Identity theft involved the actual theft of another person's true identity with the intention of obtaining a loan. All of the SARs reporting identity theft were classified as fraud for profit. Mortgage brokers originated the loans on 63.93% of the reports of identity theft. Suspected elder exploitation was described in six (9.84%) of the identity theft reports. Victims informed filers of identity theft activity in 65.57% of these reports. Filers identified the activity prior to funding the loan on 18.03% of the reports.

---

15. The IRS issues ITINs to help individuals comply with the U.S. tax laws, and to provide a means to efficiently process and account for tax returns and payments for those who do not have, nor are eligible for SSNs.

- Flipping (2.71%). All narratives describing flipping were classified as fraud for profit. Appraisal fraud was a part of fraudulent flipping on all narratives. Filers noted that mortgage brokers originated the loans on 68.75% of the narratives describing flipping.

Elaborate Mortgage Fraud Schemes

Although the numbers of SAR narratives describing elaborate mortgage fraud schemes did not constitute a particularly significant percentage of the entire sample, some of these narratives described apparent fraud for profit schemes that were notably elaborate and organized. These schemes are described below.

- Mortgage rescue schemes. Seven of the sampled narratives described fraudulent mortgage rescue schemes. Fraud perpetrators preyed on individuals threatened with foreclosure of their homes. Typically, the home owner was told that if they signed a quit claim deed for the benefit of the rescuer, the mortgage would be paid and the homeowner could continue living in the house with the promise that the property would be deeded back when the homeowner was able to obtain refinancing. The rescuer recorded the quit claim deed and then sold the property. Whereas in these instances, the borrower was the victim of the fraud, another type of mortgage rescue scheme defrauded the lender. In these cases, borrowers participated as straw buyers to purchase property and then quit claim the property back to the seller. This was considered a type of mortgage rescue scheme since typically the sellers were in default when the transfers occurred.

- "Freeman in nature" schemes. Four reports described attempted fraudulent payoffs with "Freeman in nature" arguments.[16] These arguments claimed that no money exchanged hands (i.e., the loan was merely a paper transaction), therefore there was no duty to repay the mortgage. Suspected Freeman schemes made up less than 1% of the sampled narratives, but they represent a danger to both lenders and homeowners. The reviewed Freeman schemes frequently resulted in the filing of fraudulent lien releases in county land records endangering the lender's loan security. Ultimately, homeowners who participate in these schemes lose their homes.

---

16. "Freeman in nature" arguments refer to specious arguments that avow that the funds were never loaned and therefore the borrower has no duty to repay the mortgage. These arguments rely on an unreasonable interpretation of Section 1-207 of the Uniform Commercial Code that has never been affirmed or supported by any court or governmental authority.

- <u>Asset rental.</u> Ten of the sampled narratives described suspected fraudulent attempts to temporarily inflate borrowers' assets in order to qualify them for loans. Typically, the borrower's name was added to an existing account. After the institution holding the account verified the assets in that account, the borrower's name was removed. Eight (80%) of these reports were submitted by the institutions that were requested to prepare verifications of deposit. The filers noticed that the funds were withdrawn or the names were removed shortly after a verification of deposit request was completed. These proactive reports demonstrated an awareness of this type of fraud and provided examples of successful industry efforts to identify them.

Institutions receiving verification of deposit (VOD) requests are well positioned to detect and prevent some asset rental schemes. It may be a red flag when an account holder repeatedly adds new names to an account, then drops them shortly after the bank responds to a VOD. In these cases, the account holder may have added the loan applicant's name to the account to boost the latter's (apparent) available assets. Recurring incidents of this type of asset rental suggest that the asset renter likely has a direct connection to the loan processor, either a broker or a bank insider that routinely arranges for loans. Banks tracking suspicious activity that includes VOD requests can note on their SAR the party that requests the VOD in either the subject field or the narrative, as is appropriate.

Other instances of asset rental were detected when filers noted that funds were temporarily deposited into the loan applicant's bank account for the time required to qualify for a loan. The funds came from friends or family, or even from mortgage brokers attempting to qualify an ineligible borrower. The temporary funds were withdrawn from the bank account after the loans were approved. Since these transactions only occur once, they are more difficult to detect than using the method above. However, the asset renter faces greater risk of losing his or her borrowed funds.

- <u>Fraudulent investment schemes.</u> Borrowers obtained loans for multiple properties within a short period of time. Frequently the subject properties were located in states outside the borrower's home state. The fraudulent activities generally included appraisal fraud, occupancy fraud, fraudulent property flipping, forged or fraudulent documents, and misrepresentation of assets and debts. These schemes also included borrowers participating in fraudulent real estate investment schemes by agreeing to have their personal credit used to acquire mortgages in return for a fee plus the promise of additional commissions when the property was resold. Investors were told the properties would be renovated and sold in approximately one year, and that mortgage payments would be made with rental income. The fraudulent activities generally included appraisal fraud, asset rental fraud, occupancy fraud, straw buyer, and misrepresentation of assets and debts. Ultimately the borrowers were left owing mortgages that exceeded the property value.

- <u>Creating false down payments for properties.</u> Activities included depositing advances from credit cards into bank accounts then using those funds to obtain official checks payable to a title company. The funds were later returned from the title company to the bank account. In reality, the property was obtained for no money down, while creating a false appearance to the lender that the borrower had made a down payment. Another variation reported was the disguising of purchase loans as refinance loans with no money down and possibly cash back at the time of settlement. In reality the property is transferred to the borrower at the time the "refinance" loan is closed. This type of activity increases the likelihood the borrower will default on the loan since the borrower has no financial vested interest, since their earnest money was funded by a loan.

    Lenders may find it helpful to review the HUD-1 settlement statement for disbursements to unknown individuals or entities. These disbursements may represent payments to the sellers.

- <u>Short payoff.</u> Inflated appraisals were used to obtain the subject loans. Borrowers defaulted on the loans and claimed a fraudulent hardship, such as loss of employment or illness. The borrowers further claimed they were victims of appraisal fraud and requested that the lenders accept short payoffs. The proposed payoffs were based on legitimate appraisals that were significantly less (40 to 60 percent less) than the appraisals used to obtain the loans.

- <u>Fraudulent credit reports.</u> Employees of a credit bureau changed credit reports to fraudulently improve credit profiles by removing legitimate negative information and adding positive information.

  These reports suggest that some lenders may reduce the likelihood of fraud by obtaining credit information from all three major credit bureaus.

- <u>Property Theft.</u>

  - Property was sold with the promise of granting a life estate to the seller. The deed was altered to remove the life estate provision prior to recording. The property was then resold without the life estate provision in a true arms-length transaction, and a mortgage was placed against the property. The original homeowner, the purchaser, and the subsequent mortgage holder were left to sort out the legal and financial consequences of this fraud. Sampled narratives frequently specified that victims of this type of fraud were elderly.

  - Loan applications were made in the name of deceased owners. The fraud perpetrator needs to work quickly before heirs can file wills or estate executor documents with the courts. This type of fraud is aided by rapid loan processing.

  - Individuals stole the identities of property owners to allow them to sell the property to another individual who assumed the identity of another true person. In this scheme, the existing mortgage on the property was paid off with a new mortgage. The perpetrators received the difference between the sales price and the loan payoff. Therefore, this fraud scheme is more profitable when perpetrated against homeowners with a large amount of equity, i.e., where market value exceeds the outstanding debt on the home. The legitimate homeowners discover the fraud when they are informed that their mortgage has been paid in full.

☐ ID theft of the true homeowner's identity to apply for home equity lines of credit or cash-out refinancing. "Shotgunning" is frequently a part of this fraud. In this scheme, the borrower applies for multiple loans from multiple lenders on the same property in a short period of time. This allows the identity thief to take advantage of lag time in recording the mortgages. Consequently, lenders are unable to identify the existence of the other loans. By the time the lender is aware of the other mortgages, the loan payment has already been provided. Successful applications usually result in first payment defaults.

Protective Measures

Effective Fraud Detection Measures Used by Filers

Filers reported various measures for detecting potential mortgage loan fraud involving particular examination procedures and red flag indicators. There are a variety of legitimate transactions that can raise a red flag, and the mere presence of a red flag does not automatically indicate suspicious or illicit activity. The following red flags and detection measures were derived from a review of SAR narratives describing mortgage loan fraud detection measures.

Some lending institutions rely heavily, though not exclusively, on submitting brokers to perform proper due diligence checks on the loan applicant. Sampled SAR narratives suggest that lending institutions performing independent due diligence on the borrower and conducting re-verification of documents increase their ability to detect fraud. In many cases, these checks can quickly identify document fraud. Additionally, by tracking failure rates of loans associated with particular brokers, lenders are detecting systematic abuses.

In many cases, applying simple reasonability tests are sufficient to detect fraudulent documents. For instance, a much greater than normal increase in year-to-year income or an occupational income far higher than those of others in the same line of work can present a red flag. An effective measure to detect fraudulent documents includes performing routine tests to ensure the applicant's reported Social Security and Medicare withholdings do not exceed the limits established by law.

Borrowers purchasing property described as a primary residence, but outside of their home states, or located an unreasonable commuting distance from their stated employer, could be an indication that the borrowers do not truly intend for the property to be their principal residence. This could be an indication of straw buyer involvement or that the property is intended as an investment rather than a principal residence.

Mortgage brokers or borrowers that always use the same appraiser can be a red flag for appraisal fraud in some instances.

In some cases, identity theft can be detected and prevented by ensuring that the borrower's signature matches on all documents. Sampled SAR narratives show multiple instances of alert reviewers detecting fraudulent applications by comparing document signatures and finding discrepancies. Alert loan settlement providers can also prevent ID theft by ensuring that all parties present acceptable photo identification and ensuring that all documents are signed in front of a licensed notary public.

Multiple problematic loan applications containing the same parties working in conjunction with one another may also be a red flag for organized fraud. For example, numerous transactions involving the same mortgage broker, seller, appraiser, and settlement agency may be a red flag for a fraudulent arrangement.

Other Protective Measures

As noted below in the section on "Findings Observed from Sampled Narratives," financial institutions are increasingly detecting fraud prior to loan funding.[17] The most effective financial institutions observed in the sample achieved this during the underwriting process by re-verifying the information provided in the loan application. Various federal regulatory agencies have issued guidance in response to consumer protection concerns and for reasons of safety and soundness. This guidance may provide further insight on fraud detection. Some of these documents include guidance on issuing subprime loans,[18] and best foreclosure prevention practices.[19] In addition, various state agencies have offered guidance to banks on mortgage lending practices as well.[20]

Lenders are encouraged to use the loan settlement statement (frequently the Form HUD-1) to identify clues about possible loan fraud prior to loan disbursal. Close scrutiny of where the loan funds are going could identify potential fraud prior to loan disbursement. Anecdotal reporting by law enforcement suggests that an atypically large disbursement or more of the funds to an entity or individual whose role in the transaction is not readily apparent could be an indication of fraud.

---

17. See subsection *Fraud Detection*.

18. For an example of this, see *Statement on Subprime Mortgage Lending*, issued jointly by the Office of the Comptroller of the Currency, Federal Reserve System, Federal Deposit Insurance Corporation, Office of Thrift Supervision, and National Credit Union Administration. The full document can be found at: http://www.occ.treas.gov/ftp/release/2007-64a.pdf.

19. For example, see *Foreclosure Prevention: Improving Contact with Borrowers*, Office of the Comptroller of the Currency, http://www.occ.treas.gov/cdd/Foreclosure_Prevention_Insights.pdf.

20. For instance, various guidelines can be found on the Conference of State Bank Supervisors website; see http://www.csbs.org.

Trends and Patterns in Total SARs Reporting Mortgage Loan Fraud

S ARs reporting suspected mortgage loan fraud continue to increase. This study includes SARs reporting suspected mortgage loan fraud filed between April 1, 2006 and March 31, 2007. *Figure 7* below provides a graphic depiction of the filing trend of SARs reporting suspected mortgage loan fraud.

Figure 7

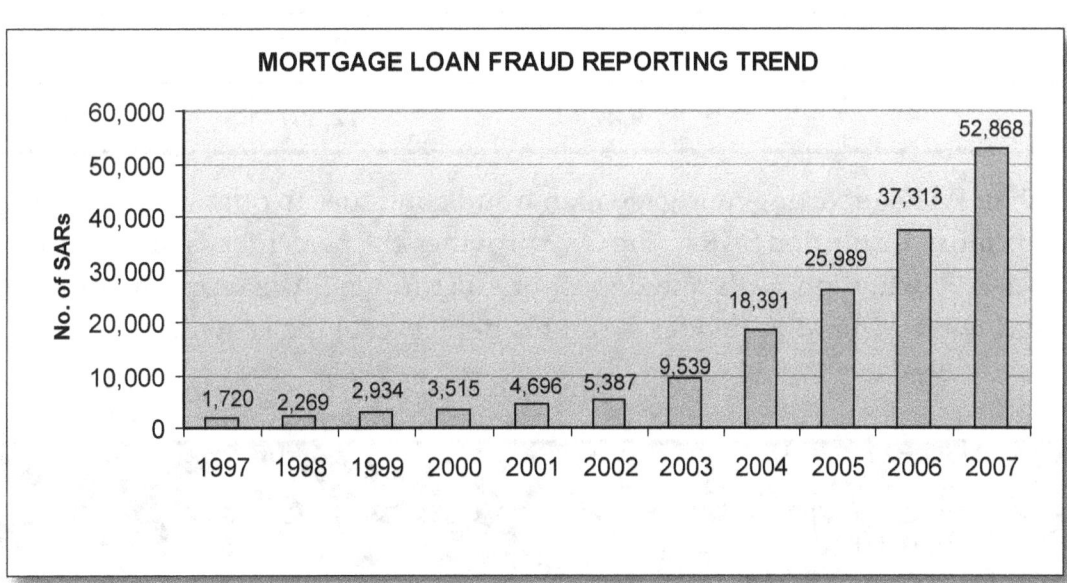

Quick Facts

- Financial institutions filed 37,313 SARs citing suspected mortgage fraud in 2006, a 44% increase from 2005.

- A comparison of 1st quarters 2006 and 2007 shows a 37% increase in SARs identifying mortgage fraud.

A comparison of SARs reporting suspected mortgage loan fraud for the first quarter of 2006 to the first quarter of 2007 revealed a growth of 36.79%.

Figure 8 provides this comparison.

FIGURE 8

COMPARISON OF 1ST QTR 2006 TO 1ST QTR 2007			
	2006	*2007*	*Percentage of Growth*
January	2,087	3,422	63.97%
February	2,301	3,522	53.06%
March	3,034	3,946	30.06%
Total	**9,428**	**12,897**	**36.79%**

Growth in SARs reporting mortgage loan fraud continues to outpace the growth of total depository institution SARs. *Figure 9* provides the percentages of growth for all depository institution SARs and depository institution SARs reporting mortgage loan fraud while *Figure 10* provides a graphic depiction of the growth.

FIGURE 9

COMPARISON OF GROWTH IN TOTAL DEPOSITORY SARs TO GROWTH IN SARs REPORTING MORTGAGE LOAN FRAUD				
Year	*Total Depository Institution SAR Filings*	*Mortgage Loan Fraud SARs*	*Growth in Total Depository SARs*	*Growth in Mortgage Loan Fraud SARs*
1996	62,388	1,318	N/A	N/A
1997	81,197	1,720	45.81%	30.50%
1998	96,521	2,269	18.87%	31.92%
1999	120,505	2,934	24.85%	29.31%

(*FIGURE 9* continued on the next page)

(FIGURE 9 continued from the previous page)

Year	Total Depository Institution SAR Filings	Mortgage Loan Fraud SARs	Growth in Total Depository SARs	Growth in Mortgage Loan Fraud SARs
2000	162,720	3,515	35.03%	19.80%
2001	203,538	4,696	25.08%	33.60%
2002	273,823	5,387	34.53%	14.71%
2003	288,343	9,539	5.30%	77.07%
2004	381,671	18,391	32.37%	92.80%
2005	522,655	25,989	36.94%	41.31%
2006	567,080	37,313	7.75%	43.57%
TOTAL	**2,757,367**	**113,071**		

FIGURE 10

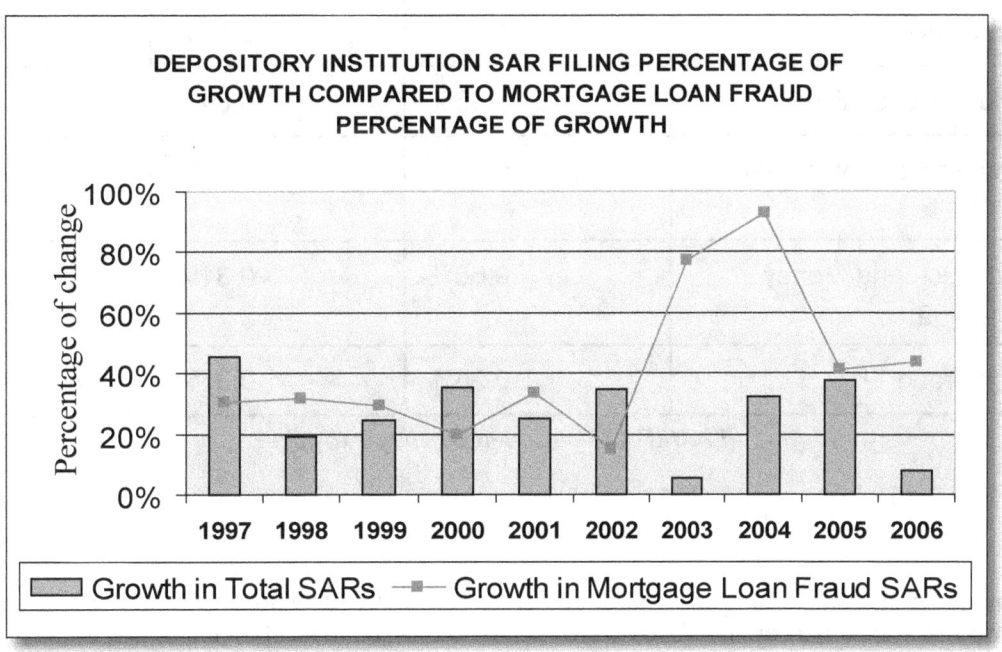

Characterizations of Suspicious Activity

Many reports included more than one characterization of suspicious activity in addition to mortgage loan fraud.[21] False statement was the most reported suspicious activity in conjunction with mortgage loan fraud. *Figure 11* reveals secondary characterizations of suspicious activities reported in conjunction with mortgage loan fraud and compares this to percentages from the preceding ten years. Reports of identity theft doubled from 2% to 4% of the SARs filed. Although the overall numbers of reports were small, computer intrusion also saw a significant percentage increase.

FIGURE 11

COMPARISON OF INITIAL AND UPDATED REPORTS BY CHARACTERIZATION OF SUSPICIOUS ACTIVITY			
Characterization of Suspicious Activity	*Updated Report (4/06 – 3/07)*	*Initial Report (4/96 – 3/06)*	*Percentage of Change*
Mortgage Loan Fraud	100.00%	100.00%	0.00%
False Statement	29.43%	18.58%	58.42%
Other	4.65%	3.80%	22.36%
Identity Theft	4.17%	2.13%	95.62%
Consumer Loan Fraud	1.48%	0.84%	74.99%
Misuse of Position or Self Dealing	0.71%	1.47%	-51.79%
BSA/Structuring/Money Laundering	0.60%	0.31%	95.25%
Check Fraud	0.26%	0.31%	-14.28%

(FIGURE 11 continued on the next page)

---

21. In our examination in mortgage loan fraud SARs, we identified 69 SARs with multiple activity characterizations that contained one or more mischaracterizations of financial crimes, including primary activities and those secondary to mortgage loan fraud. As the full 69 only reflect about one-tenth of one percent of all mortgage loan fraud SARs, the errors are not statistically significant.

(FIGURE 11 continued from the previous page)

Characterization of Suspicious Activity	Updated Report (4/06 – 3/07)	Initial Report (4/96 – 3/06)	Percentage of Change
Counterfeit Instrument	0.19%	0.26%	-26.97%
Defalcation/Embezzlement	0.15%	0.45%	-66.77%
Computer Intrusion	0.13%	0.04%	214.01%
Wire Transfer Fraud	0.12%	0.20%	-39.89%
Mysterious Disappearance[22]	n/a	n/a	n/a
Counterfeit Check	0.07%	0.08%	-17.55%
Check Kiting	0.05%	0.07%	-37.73%
Credit Card Fraud	0.04%	0.07%	-42.97%
Bribery/Gratuity	0.03%	0.08%	-64.14%
Terrorist Financing[23]	n/a	n/a	n/a
Debit Card Fraud	0.00%	0.03%	-100.00%
Commercial Loan Fraud	0.00%	0.49%	-100.00%
Counterfeit Credit/Debit Card	0.00%	0.01%	-100.00%

---

22. Approximately half of the 30 reports characterized as mysterious disappearance appear to be misclassified. These mischaracterizations likely resulted from human or computer errors. For example, several SARs specified multiple activities including mortgage loan fraud, terrorist financing, identity theft, mysterious disappearance, but for all these SARs the activities were in fact attempts to evade filing thresholds for BSA documents, as gleaned from the filers' thorough narrative descriptions.

23. Although twelve SARs listed terrorist financing in conjunction with mortgage loan fraud, a close review of those SARs revealed that all these reports were mischaracterized.

Primary Federal Regulators

Figure 12 displays the primary federal regulators identified in the reports of mortgage loan fraud.[24] National banks with offices located throughout the country made up the largest group of lenders reporting mortgage loan fraud. The Office of the Comptroller of the Currency (OCC) is the primary regulator for national banks. National banks filed about a third of the total reports.

Figure 12

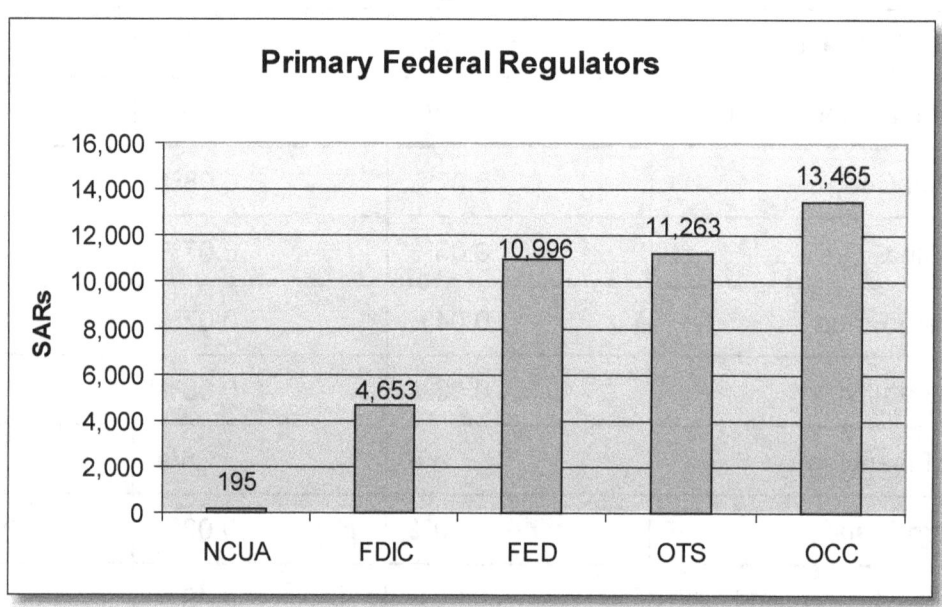

The Office of Federal Housing Enterprise Oversight (OFHEO) is the federal regulator for two government sponsored enterprises — Fannie Mae and Freddie Mac. In 2006, OFHEO adopted a final rule which established a process for the enterprises' reporting of possible mortgage fraud to OFHEO and corresponding reporting to FinCEN. As this process continues to develop, FinCEN will continue to monitor these filings for developing trends.

Quick Facts

- The top five subject states for reported mortgage fraud were California, Florida, Illinois, Georgia, and Texas.

- SAR filings on suspected mortgage fraud subjects increased by more than 50% in ten subject states over the previous year.

---

24. Some SARs did not indicate the primary regulator.

Top Filing Institutions

In all, 788 depository institutions and their subsidiaries filed 40,781 SARs on suspected mortgage loan fraud (6.8% of total SARs filed in the same period) during the period April 1, 2006 through March 31, 2007. The top 10 filers that listed mortgage loan fraud as a category account for 61% of these SARs, while the top 25 filers account for 87% of the total.

Fraud Locations

SARs contain data fields for subject addresses, the filer's main office address, and the filer's branch address where the suspicious activity was discovered. Because the subject address provides the best source for identifying geographic locations of real estate involved in mortgage loan fraud, this study identified the location of the fraud by the subject address. This is because most residential mortgage loan applicants intend to reside on the property used to secure the loan. In the SARs reviewed in this study, suspicious activity occurred in, or was otherwise associated with, all 50 states, the District of Columbia, Puerto Rico, and American Samoa.

Figure 13 provides the top 20 subject states by the number of depository institution SARs filed in 2006 along with a comparison to the 2005 filings and the percentage of change for the two years. *Figure 13* also provides the per capita income and state ranking for those 20 states based on per capita income. The top five reported subject address states were California, Florida, Illinois, Georgia, and Texas. This represented a change in position from the initial report where the top five subject address states were California, Florida, Georgia, Texas and Illinois. Illinois moved from fifth position to third and Georgia and Texas moved from third and fourth to fourth and fifth positions. New Jersey, Arizona and Ohio replaced Ohio, North Carolina and Washington in the seventh through tenth positions, respectively. Note that twelve of these states were ranked within the top twenty U.S. per capita income states.

FIGURE 13

		TOP 20 SUBJECT STATES[25]			
	(Number of SARs Indicating a Listed Subject is a Resident in the State)				
State	**2006 Depository Institution SARs**	**2005 Depository Institution SARs**	**Percentage Of Change**	**2006 Per Capita Income (Projected)[26]**	**Rank In U.S. (per capita income)**
California	8,109	4,734	71.29%	$38,956	11
Florida	3,552	2,321	53.04%	$35,798	20
Illinois	2,477	1,409	75.80%	$38,215	13
Georgia	2,265	1,770	27.97%	$31,891	38
Texas	2,185	1,557	40.33%	$34,257	25
New York	1,797	1,228	46.34%	$42,392	5

(FIGURE 13 continued on the next page)

---

25. This table shows the total number of SARs per state, where the SARs included the subject's address within that state. As some SARs indicate subjects in two or more states, these particular SARs may be counted multiple times in this table. Total state filings when listed by subject, as here, do not match the total number of SARs filed for the reviewed period.

26. Per capita income and state ranking obtained from the U.S. Department of Commerce, Bureau of Economic Analysis, www.bea.gov/index.htm.

(FIGURE 13 continued from the previous page)

State	2006 Depository Institution SARs	2005 Depository Institution SARs	Percentage Of Change	2006 Per Capita Income (Projected)	Rank In U.S. (per capita income)
Michigan	1,671	1,103	51.50%	$33,847	27
New Jersey	1,119	771	45.14%	$46,344	2
Arizona	1,050	706	48.73%	$31,458	39
Ohio	957	765	25.10%	$33,338	29
Virginia	818	581	40.79%	$39,173	9
Colorado	817	687	18.92%	$39,186	8
Maryland	803	573	40.14%	$44,077	4
Minnesota	758	426	77.93%	$38,712	12
North Carolina	644	605	6.45%	$32,234	36
Indiana	640	435	47.13%	$32,526	33
Pennsylvania	635	553	14.83%	$36,680	18
Missouri	605	487	24.23%	$32,705	31
Washington	584	480	21.67%	$37,423	14
Nevada	562	361	55.68%	$37,089	17

Figure 14 provides the percentage of change in reporting for all subject states along with data from the U.S. Department of Commerce, Bureau of Economics reporting the per capita income and state rankings for 2006 (projected). Although Alaska had only 38 SARs reporting mortgage loan fraud in 2006, it was the state with the largest growth in reports of mortgage loan fraud by percentage increase. States with negative growth included South Dakota, Iowa, Vermont, South Carolina, New Mexico, and Kansas. Eleven of the twenty states showing the greatest increase in reported subjects were ranked within the top twenty states for per capita income.

FIGURE 14

PERCENTAGE OF CHANGE IN REPORTED SUBJECT STATES

State	2006 Depository Institution SARs	2005 Depository Institution SARs	Percentage Of Change	2006 Per Capita Income (Projected)[27]	Rank In U.S.(per capita income)
Alaska	38	8	375.00%	$37,271	16
Rhode Island	164	47	248.94%	$37,388	15
Minnesota	758	426	77.93%	$38,712	12
Illinois	2,477	1,409	75.80%	$38,215	13
Massachusetts	477	276	72.83%	$45,877	3
California	8,109	4,734	71.29%	$38,956	11
Mississippi	150	92	63.04%	$26,535	50
Nevada	562	361	55.68%	$37,089	17
Florida	3,552	2,321	53.04%	$35,798	20
Michigan	1,671	1,103	51.50%	$33,847	27
Arizona	1,050	706	48.73%	$31,458	39

(FIGURE 14 continued on the next page)

27. Per capita income and state ranking obtained from the U.S. Department of Commerce, Bureau of Economic Analysis, www.bea.gov/index.htm.

*(**FIGURE 14** continued from the previous page)*

State	2006 Depository Institution SARs	2005 Depository Institution SARs	Percentage Of Change	2006 Per Capita Income (Projected)	Rank In U.S.(per capita income)
Indiana	640	435	47.13%	$32,526	33
Idaho	148	101	46.53%	$29,952	43
New York	1,797	1,228	46.34%	$42,392	5
Arkansas	95	65	46.15%	$27,935	48
Wisconsin	495	340	45.59%	$34,701	22
New Jersey	1,119	771	45.14%	$46,344	2
Connecticut	252	174	44.83%	$49,852	1
Maine	42	29	44.83%	$32,348	34
Alabama	242	169	43.20%	$31,295	40
Virginia	818	581	40.79%	$39,173	9
Texas	2,185	1,557	40.33%	$34,257	25
Maryland	803	573	40.14%	$44,077	4
Utah	414	312	32.69%	$29,108	47
District of Columbia	67	51	31.37%	$55,755	--
Tennessee	483	376	28.46%	$32,304	35
Georgia	2,265	1,770	27.97%	$31,891	38
New Hampshire	61	48	27.08%	$39,311	7
Montana	33	26	26.92%	$30,688	42
Ohio	957	765	25.10%	$33,338	29
Missouri	605	487	24.23%	$32,705	31

*(**FIGURE 14** continued on the next page)*

(FIGURE 14 continued from the previous page)

State	2006 Depository Institution SARs	2005 Depository Institution SARs	Percentage Of Change	2006 Per Capita Income (Projected)	Rank In U.S.(per capita income)
Louisiana	222	181	22.65%	$30,952	41
Washington	584	480	21.67%	$37,423	14
Hawaii	73	60	21.67%	$36,299	19
Nebraska	63	52	21.15%	$34,397	23
Colorado	817	687	18.92%	$39,186	8
Wyoming	14	12	16.67%	$40,676	6
Delaware	50	43	16.28%	$39,022	10
Oklahoma	195	168	16.07%	$32,210	37
Pennsylvania	635	553	14.83%	$36,680	18
Kentucky	162	146	10.96%	$29,352	46
North Carolina	644	605	6.45%	$32,234	36
Oregon	260	257	1.17%	$33,666	28
West Virginia	34	34	0.00%	$27,897	49
North Dakota	6	6	0.00%	$32,552	32
Kansas	172	175	-1.71%	$34,743	21
New Mexico	120	126	-4.76%	$29,673	44
South Carolina	376	405	-7.16%	$29,515	45
Vermont	11	12	-8.33%	$34,264	24
Iowa	87	95	-8.42%	$33,236	30
South Dakota	9	12	-25.00%	$33,929	26

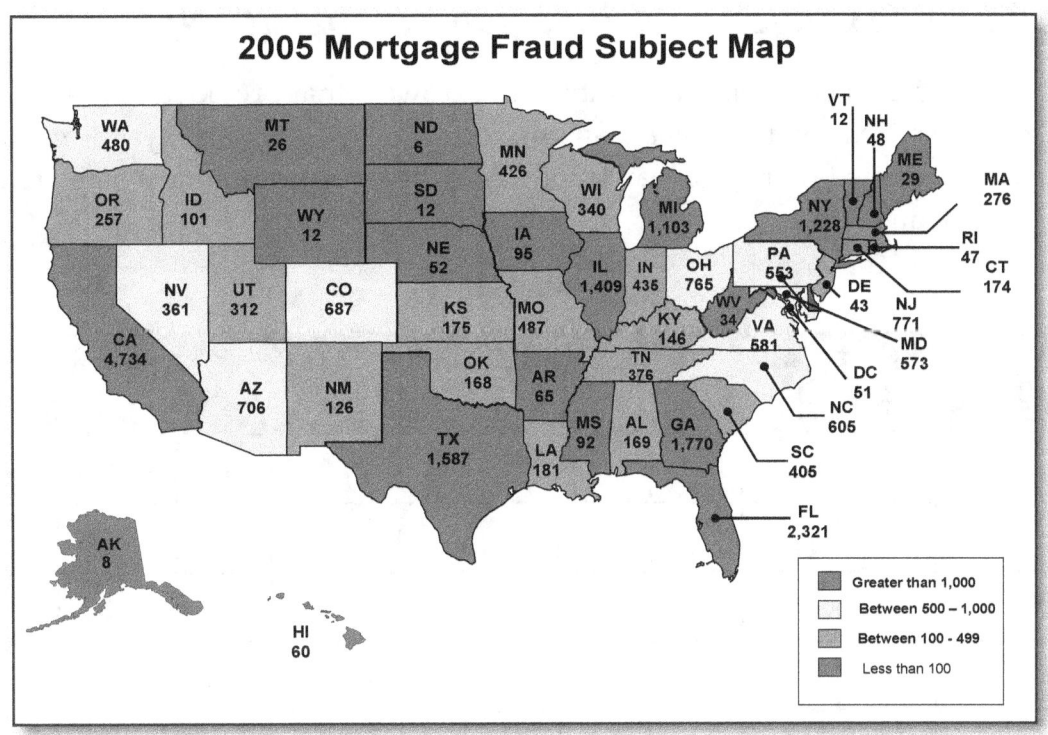

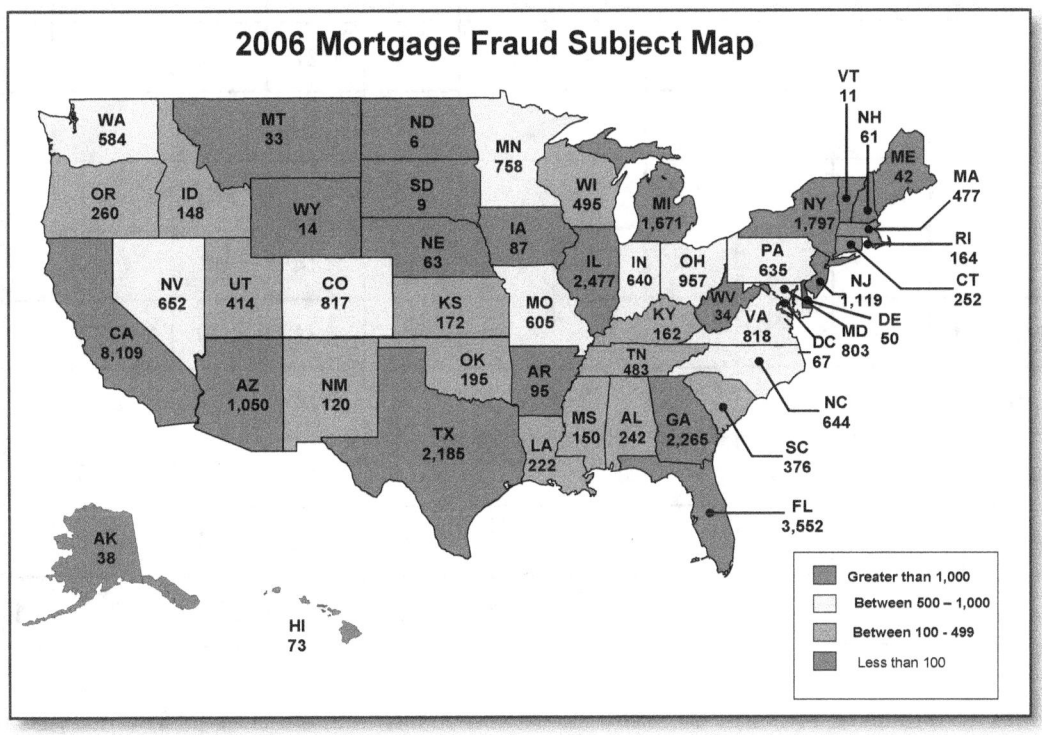

The maps above depict the volume of SARs identifying subject states associated with suspected mortgage loan fraud for 2005 and 2006.

Individual Taxpayer Identification Number (ITIN)

Filers reported an increase in the number of borrowers that provided ITINs,[28] often represented as SSNs, on mortgage loan applications. *Figure 15* displays the growing number of suspected mortgage loan fraud SARs reporting individuals who are associated with an ITIN.

FIGURE 15

MORTGAGE LOAN FRAUD SARs REPORTING USE OF ITINs									
	1999	**2000**	**2001**	**2002**	**2003**	**2004**	**2005**	**2006**	**2007**[29]	**TOTAL**
January				1		1	20	44	35	**101**
February						1	20	43	52	**116**
March				1		3	16	66	110	**196**
April					4	1	7	39	137	**188**
May	1			4	5	2	27	42	62	**143**
June						0	24	43	131	**198**
July						8	31	33	41	**113**
August				1		19	14	41	29	**104**
September						7	31	29	60	**127**
October					1	4	24	52	77	**158**
November		2	2			14	50	39	43	**150**
December			1		3	22	33	29	79	**167**
Total	**1**	**2**	**3**	**7**	**13**	**82**	**297**	**500**	**856**	**1,761**

28. An ITIN is a nine-digit number issued by the U.S. Internal Revenue Service (IRS) to individuals who are required for U.S. tax purposes to have a U.S. taxpayer identification number but who do not have, and are not eligible to obtain, a social security number (SSN). See IRS Discussion of ITINs at http://www.irs.gov. For additional compliance guidance, see *The SAR Activity Review: Trends, Tips & Issues*, Issue 11, Section 4, "Tips on SAR Form Preparation and Filing," at http://www.fincen.gov/sarreviewissue11.pdf.

29. Totals for November and December 2007 may not be complete due to processing.

Figure 16 provides a graphic depiction of the filing trend for reports of individuals associated with both an ITIN and a SSN.

FIGURE 16

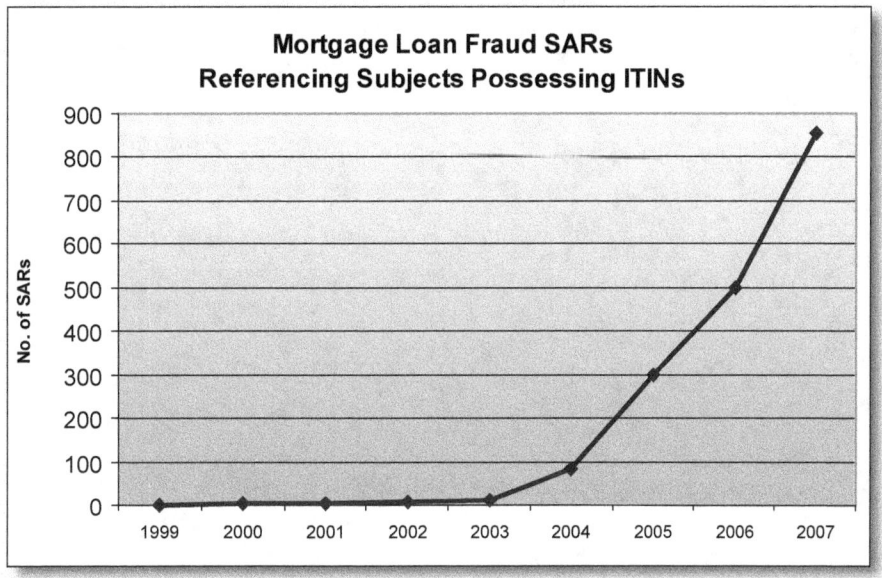

Findings Observed from Sampled Narratives

A sample of 1,769 depository institution SAR narratives was reviewed to identify additional trends and patterns reported in those narratives. Comparisons to the findings in the FinCEN report published November 2006 were made whenever possible. The percentages presented frequently do not add up to 100% because not all narratives provided sufficient information to determine classifications such as loan types, fraud types, and activities.

Types of Fraud

Mortgage fraud is generally divided into two broad categories: fraud for housing and fraud for profit. Fraud for housing was the most common type reported in the sampled narratives (60%).[30] Fraud for profit was reported in just over 36% of the sampled narratives.

---

30. For this study, occurrences are classified as fraud for profit in SARs where 1) the filers specifically state their suspicion is about fraud for profit, 2) the filers do not specifically state it is fraud for housing, 3) the narrative describes subjects other than the borrower as suspected primary participants, 4) the filer specifically notes possible occupancy fraud, or 5) the suspected fraudulent loan is not a first mortgage. Absent any of these criteria, other reports are classified as fraud for housing, when the filer named the borrower as a subject.

Figures 17 and *18* displays the types of participants in these fraud categories and show the frequency of their mention in each category.

FIGURE 17

Participant	Percentage of Participants in SARs Describing Fraud For Profit	Percentage of Participants in SARs Describing Fraud For Housing
Mortgage Broker	62.07%	58.55%
Borrower	60.66%	87.06%
Appraiser	23.04%	7.46%
Investor	14.42%	0.00%
Seller	7.52%	0.76%
Settlement Agency/Notary	2.66%	1.13%
Insider (Loan Officer)	2.35%	1.13%
Correspondent Lender	1.72%	1.42%

COMPARISON OF FRAUD FOR PROFIT AND HOUSING BY PARTICIPANT

FIGURE 18

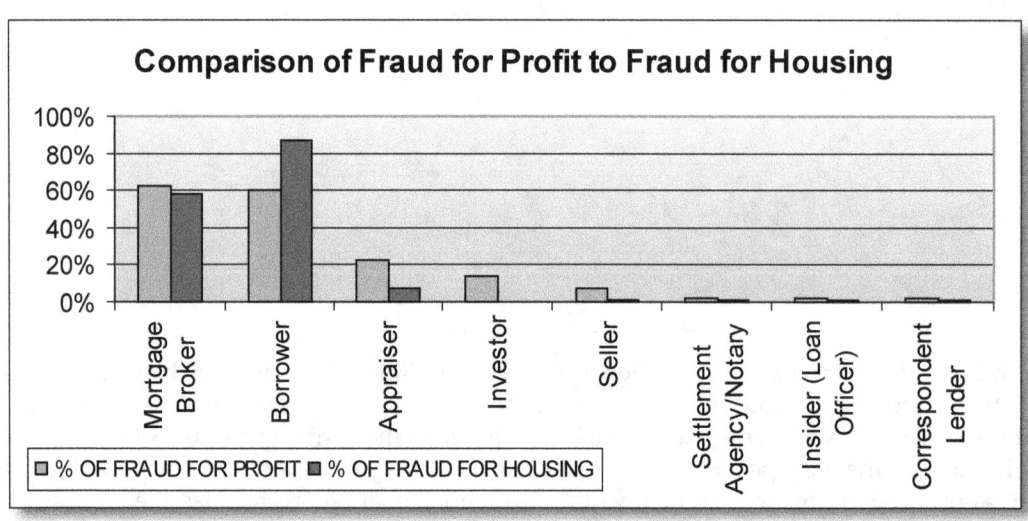

Reports describing suspected fraud for housing referenced purchase loans most often, followed by refinance, 2nd trust, and home equity loans. All reports regarding construction loans described suspected fraud for profit. Home equity loans had the second highest percentage of fraud for profit with 2nd trust, refinance, and purchase loans showing the next highest percentages.

Figure 19 illustrates a comparison of the type of fraud by loan type as seen in the sampled narratives.

FIGURE 19

LOAN TYPE COMPARISON FOR TYPE OF FRAUD				
Loan Type	Profit	Percentage of Loan Type	Housing	Percentage of Loan Type
Purchase	440	34.00%	840	64.91%
Refinance	93	45.15%	112	54.37%
2nd Trust	20	47.62%	22	52.38%
Home Equity	38	61.29%	24	38.71%
Construction	19	100.00%	0	0%
Total	610		998	

Loan Types

Loans for purchasing houses, either for a primary residence, second home, or investment, were the most commonly reported loan types detailing suspected fraud, at 72.75%. Other types of loans reported were: refinance (12.04%), home equity (3.5%), 2nd trust (2.37%), and construction (1.07%). Some significant changes were found by comparing loan types reported in FinCEN's previous mortgage fraud report to loan types reported during the update period. The percentage of fraudulent construction loans and purchase loans reported experienced a decrease while reports of fraud in 2nd trust, refinance, and home equity loans increased.

Figure 20 displays the comparison.

FIGURE 20

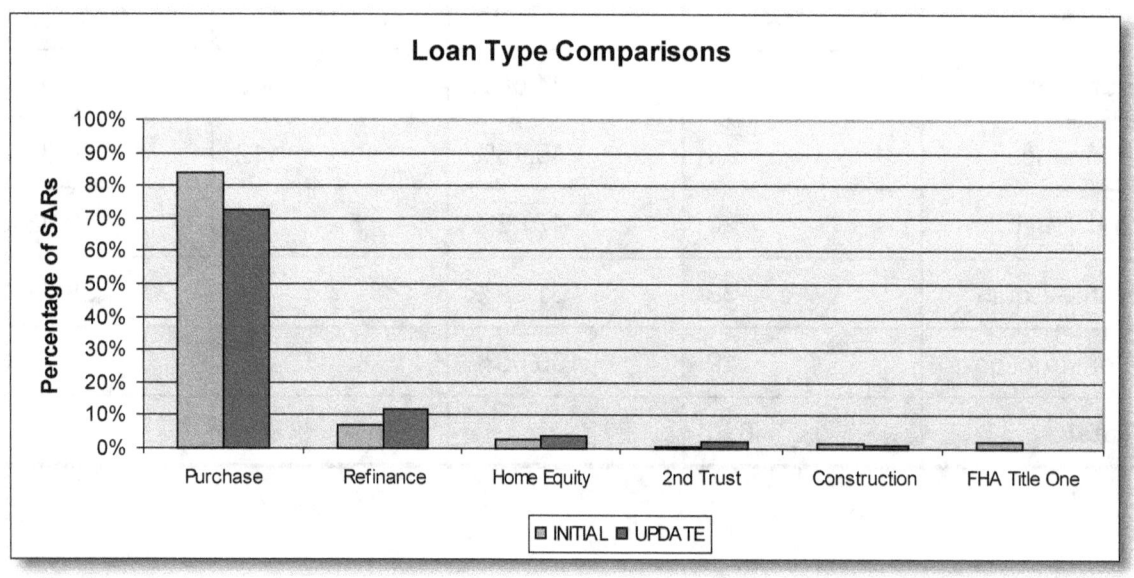

Filers specified that loans were subprime in 79 SARs (0.19%) for the reviewed period. Without this specification, it is not possible to determine whether mortgages described in the remaining SARs were subprime loans.

Filers did not identify any FHA Title One loans in the sampled narratives reviewed for this update report. It is unknown if there was a decrease in reports of fraud in FHA Title One loans, or if the filers simply did not identify the loans as such. Filers did note that six purchase loans and one refinance loan were FHA insured loans.

Figure 21 provides a comparison of loan types for the initial and updated reports.

FIGURE 21

REPORT COMPARISON			
Loan Type	Initial Report	Updated Report	Percentage Of Change
Purchase	83.65%	72.75%	-13.03%
Refinance	7.21%	12.04%	66.99%
Home Equity	2.66%	3.50%	31.76%
2nd Trust	0.38%	2.37%	524.80%
Construction	1.52%	1.07%	-29.34%
FHA Title One	1.90%	0.00%	-100.00%

Filers noted in the sampled narratives that 54 (25.35%) of the refinance loans were "cash-out refinance." Additionally, filers noted that 7.41% of the cash-out refinance loans were early defaults; half of those were first payment defaults.

Early Payment Default

Filers reported that early payment defaults triggered suspicion that loans may have been obtained through fraudulent methods in 71 (4%) of the

Quick Facts

- Early payment defaults were indicated in only 4% of sampled narratives.

- Suspected fraud detected during foreclosure rose by 23%.

sampled narratives. Twenty-five (35.21%) of those narratives specified a first payment default. Filers reported early payment defaults were moderately more common in fraud for profit (57.75%) than fraud for housing (42.25%).

Figure 22 displays the types of loans where early payment defaults were detected.

FIGURE 22

EARLY DEFAULT BY LOAN TYPE		
Loan Type	*No. Of SARs*	*Percentage Of Loan Type*
Purchase	53	4.12%
Refinance	13	6.10%
2nd Trust	3	7.14%
Home Equity	2	3.23%

Figure 23 provides a comparison of suspected fraud for profit and fraud for housing by loan type.

FIGURE 23

EARLY PAYMENT DEFAULT COMPARISON BY FRAUD TYPE		
Type of Loan	*Profit*	*Housing*
Purchase	29	24
Refinance	9	4
Home Equity	2	0
2nd Trust	1	2
Total	**41**	**30**

Stated Income/Low Document or No Document Loans

Filers reported in 69 (3.90%) of the sampled narratives that the reviewed loans were Stated Income, Low Document or No Document loans. Mortgage brokers originated nearly 80% of these loans. Filers reported that fraud for housing (49.28%) and fraud for profit (47.83%) were nearly equally represented in these loans. Nearly 9% of these loans were early payment defaults; 50% of those were first payment defaults.

Figure 24 below displays the types of loans granted as low/no document or stated income.

FIGURE 24

STATED INCOME/LOW or NO DOCUMENT LOANS		
Loan Type	*Low Doc/Stated Income*	*Percentage Of Low Doc*
Purchase	55	79.71%
Refinance	12	17.39%
Home Equity	2	2.90%
2nd Trust	0	0.00%
Construction	0	0.00%

Fraud Detection

Filers reported they detected the possibility of fraud in various phases of the loan process: pre-finance, post finance audit, loan default; and through reports by victims, law enforcement, and even the borrowers themselves. SARs noting detection during post finance audits also reported that the loans were performing and current at the time the SARs were filed.

Figure 25 below displays a comparison of when the suspected fraud was detected in FinCEN's initial report to when it was detected in the updated report. The comparison shows that there was nearly a 50% increase in the percentage of SARs specifying fraud detection prior to loan funding. SARs reporting that the filers detected possible fraud after loan defaults increased nearly 23%. As shown in *Figure 25*, fraud detection by law enforcement increased by 71%. Filers reported they were contacted by law enforcement to report that their customer was under investigation for loan fraud or to subpoena records for their investigation.

FIGURE 25

REPORT COMPARISON			
When Detected	*Initial Report*	*Updated Report*	*Percentage Of Change*
Post Finance Audit	59.13%	42.34%	-28.39%
Pre-Finance	20.72%	30.98%	49.50%
Default	11.88%	14.58%	22.71%
Victim	2.38%	3.79%	59.48%
Law Enforcement	0.76%	1.30%	70.95%
Borrower	0.57%	1.07%	87.61%

As shown in *Figure 25* above, there was a more than 59% increase in detection through contact by victims of fraud, mostly identity theft cases. One explanation for the increase in victim reports could be greater consumer awareness of identity theft and greater use of free annual credit bureau checks, resulting in more frequent credit report checks.

Figure 25 also shows a nearly 88% increase in the reports of borrowers contacting lenders to request a change in the Social Security Number associated with their loans. The borrowers were, in effect, revealing that they used a fraudulent Social Security Number at the time the loan was initiated.

Securities and Futures Industries (SAR-SFs)

I n this updated study, FinCEN also examined Suspicious Activity Reports by securities firms involved in the issuance and sale of mortgage-backed securities. Eighteen filers submitted 36 Suspicious Activity Report by the Securities and Futures Industries (SAR-SF) forms indicating activity involving suspected mortgage loan fraud from the mandated reporting date of January 1, 2003 through May 1, 2007. These reports were retrieved using narrative searches for the terms: "securitized loans," "mortgage loan," within three words of "pooled investment," "real estate securities," "collateralized mortgage," "mortgage insurance," "sub-prime" and "fraud" within three words of "mortgage."[31]

These SAR-SFs reported the following activities:

- Asset fraud. Filers reported that account statements provided as proof of a borrower's assets had been fraudulently altered. This fraud was discovered when lenders requested re-verifications of the account statements.

- Securities accounts containing proceeds from possible mortgage fraud. Filers reported that individuals identified in news media articles as either suspected or convicted of mortgage loan fraud held accounts with the filers. No filers were able to confirm if the accounts were funded with proceeds from the fraudulent activity. Accounts held by these subjects were included in on-going due diligence programs.

- Life insurance policies possibly funded with proceeds from possible mortgage fraud. Two life insurance companies reported that their clients were identified in news media as being associated with mortgage loan fraud. The filers could not determine if the policies were funded with proceeds derived from mortgage fraud schemes. The news articles were reviewed as part of on-going due diligence programs.

---

31. The searches did not retrieve SAR-SFs reporting fraud in securitized or pooled mortgages.

Conclusion

A review of SARs suggests that although reports of suspected mortgage loan fraud continue to grow, the filers appeared to be initiating more stringent practices to prevent it. Although reports of mortgage loan fraud increased, a higher percentage of filers over previous years indicated detection of potential fraud earlier in the loan process. Reports that were reviewed demonstrated due diligence measures strengthened, at least in part, by practicing a thorough verification of data received from third parties. Consequently, the reviewed SAR filings showed a pre-funding fraud detection rate of nearly 31%, an improvement of ten percentage points over the previous years.

Narrative details in the reviewed SARs identified mortgage brokers as the loan originators for the majority of the suspected fraudulent loans; 1,025 of 1,769 narratives (nearly 58%) disclosed that the loans were originated by mortgage brokers. Details from sampled narratives identified depository institution filers as loan originators in 179 SARs (10%). Of those SARs, the fraud was detected prior to loan financing on 60 SARs (nearly 34%). Since mortgage brokers are not required to file suspicious activity reports, the number of applications rejected by mortgage brokers for suspected mortgage fraud can not be estimated from SAR filings.

www.ingramcontent.com/pod-product-compliance
Lightning Source LLC
Chambersburg PA
CBHW081234170526
45165CB00009B/3054